AF255768

bush
PUBLISHING
& associates

GOD OF VICTORY

Daily Devotional Poems

GOD OF VICTORY

Daily Devotional Poems

By Matthew Wallace

bush
PUBLISHING
& associates

Dedication

This book is dedicated to my LORD and Savior, Jesus Christ.

Each Gospel poem was written through the inspiration of the Holy Spirit. Every poem uniquely expresses my love and devotion to Jesus.

I pray that these poems open the spiritual eyes of each reader so they will understand that God is an awesome God. He is the God of salvation, the God of healing, and the God of victory.

Through His Word, He answers our prayers in power.

Bible Scripture quotes are from the *New King James Version*.

Endorsements

If you desire to be uplifted and inspired, then *GOD OF VICTORY* by Matthew Wallace is a must-read.

As a friend in Christ and mentor to many, Matthew sets the bar high in Christ-inspired excellence. His lifestyle is a beautiful example. This book of 45 Poems will bring blessings of victory, healing, and the eternal hope of salvation.

The endorsement of this treasure trove of Holy Spirit-inspired poems is an honor. Get your copy today and let the powerful words in *GOD OF VICTORY* show you the way to achieve your dreams.

Erykah Gonzalez
Sister-in-Christ, Educator, & Entrepreneur

#

"Wholehearted" is a word that perfectly describes the ministry of Matthew Wallace. He is not only my brother in Christ, he is a friend of Jesus! Matthew answered the call to "feed my sheep" with great enthusiasm and spiritual fervor. Carrying the heart of the Good Shepherd, he cares for the continual nourishment and growth of the flock. For years he has faithfully distributed daily Bible studies inspired by the Holy Spirit to those who were hungry for the LORD.

Matthew has the gift of faith and a persevering spirit found in the overcoming church. He has not neglected the gifts God has deposited in him. Because of his faithfulness, they have been gracefully multiplied in glory. Each new day is a fresh opportunity to serve the LORD and worship Him in Spirit and in Truth.

"GOD OF VICTORY" captures the heart of this book. Each poem is a pure expression of thankfulness to his Savior and a glimpse of the triumphant power found in the Gospel. As you read each of these poems, you are reading from the life of a living epistle. He is truly a new creation and wants you to know the freedom that he enjoys in Christ Jesus.

Jennifer Galey, Author

\#

I highly recommend this book, *GOD OF VICTORY*, written by Matthew Wallace. He has an amazing heart and hunger for God. I believe that this book will bring a "fire and passion" in your heart and help you fall more in love with Jesus!!!!

Tom Dillingham, Senior Pastor
CommonGround Church, Tulsa, OK

\#

Matthew is a one-of-a-kind person and mentor. He is a great encourager and a wonderful writer. He will go far in his career as a writer and a lover of God. Lastly, his poems in *GOD OF VICTORY* are inspiring.

For Matthew Wallace, by Melissa Poole

\#

I met Mr. Wallace some time ago in my journey through life, and he has encouraged me to move forward in many matters. Mr. Wallace loves to help others understand God's word and how it applies to the world they are living in. He is a great man of God.

Marviena Gibbs

Introduction

I have been a born-again Christian since April 15, 1979. With each poem, you will find an applicable Scripture, and additional Bible verses are referenced for further study. I refer to the collection as "Gospel Poems" because each poem reflects the message of salvation we find throughout the Bible. As I was praying, and meditating on the good word of God, the Holy Spirit spoke the words of each poem to me. All Scripture quotations are taken from the *King James Version* of the Bible.

Psalm 22:3, Psalm 100:4, Hebrews 12:28, Psalm 95:1-3.

Psalm 22:3 "But thou art holy, O thou that inhabitest the praises of Israel."

Psalm 100:4 "Enter his gates with thanksgiving and his courts with praise! Give thanks to him; bless his name!"

Hebrews 12:28-29 "Wherefore we receiving a kingdom which cannot be moved, let us have grace, whereby we may serve God acceptably with reverence and godly fear." *29* "For our God is a consuming fire."

Table of Contents

DAY ONE

A Brand New Season

Isaiah 43:18-19

"Remember ye, not the former things, neither consider the things of old. Behold, I will do a new thing; now it shall spring forth; shall ye not know it? I will even make a way in the wilderness, and rivers in the desert."

#

It's a Brand New Season. It's a Brand New Day. Never seen these Blessings coming my way.

It's a Brand New Season. It's a Brand New Day. The Goodness of the Lord. Just keeps Getting Better Every Day.

It's a Brand New Season. It's a Brand New Day. The Goodness of the Lord....Chasing My Fears Away.

It's a Brand New Season. It's a Brand New Day. Never seen Blessings are coming my way. His Goodness and Mercy just keep getting Better every Day.

I Lift Up My Hands

Psalm 100:4

"Enter into his gates with thanksgiving, and into his courts with praise: be thankful unto him, and bless his name."

\#

I lift up my hands. I lift up my eyes…to behold your majesty.…the skies of your sovereignty.

Your kingdom authority shines through every star. God, Your lovingkindness is better than life.

My Lips will sing your praise …. Sing your Praise.

O Holy Are you Lord.

My heart, my soul.…I lift my hands. I lift my eyes… gaze at your beauty, Lord. I worship your majesty…gaze at your beauty.…behold your majesty…gaze at your beauty…to see your beauty.

I Praise You. I Worship You.

Scripture Reading about Praising God:
Psalm 22:3, Isaiah 60:18, Hebrews 12:28, Psalm 95:1-2.

DAY THREE

My Strength Is In You, Lord

Psalm 28:7

"The Lord is my strength and my shield; my heart trusted in him, and I am helped: therefore my heart rejoiceth; and with my song I will praise him."

\#

My strength is in You. God, my hope is in You. You hold my life In your hands. The Holy Spirit now lives inside of me. Your Holy Power Has set me free.

You always give me joy….Joy unspeakable. God, my life is in your hands. All my strength comes from knowing you. I love you, Lord. I worship and I adore You. Your strength, Lord, is never-failing.

Wonderful Savior…God of Salvation. Awesome are you, my God!

My Strength is in Knowing you. All my hope is in You. You give me joy for my sorrow.

Your Word brings me hope for tomorrow. Lord, it is You that I will always follow all the days of my life.

MY PRAYER

1 John 5:14-15

"And this is the confidence that we have in him, that, if we ask anything according to his will, he heareth us. And if we know that he hear us, whatsoever we ask, we know that we have the petitions that we desired of him."

\#

Lord, I call out to You…and You are there. You are worthy to be praised. You always hear my prayer. You are always there.

Lord, You always appear on the scene. When I am in trouble…Your miracle-working power is available….every minute, every hour. God, You always hear my prayer.

Righteous God. You are a righteous King, who always answers prayer. I just want to say thank you…from the bottom of my heart…I express my thanks to You, Lord. You are the God who answers prayer… my prayer. You are always there for me.

Scripture Reading On Prayer:
1 Chronicles 16:11, 2 Chronicles 6:21, Thessalonians 5:16.

I'm a New Creation

"Therefore if any man be in Christ, he is a new creature: old things are passed away; behold, all things are become new." 2 Corinthians 5:17

\#

I am a new creation, in Christ Jesus. I am a brand new man, now I am cleansed by the blood of Jesus.

I am a new creation. I am a brand new man. I am born again. The precious blood of Jesus washed away my sins.

I am a new creation. I am a brand new man. I am born again.

You saved my life. You made my life new. Now my life is in You. Now I am born again and my life is in Your hands.

I am a new creation. I am a brand new man. I am born again, JESUS, now You are my best friend.

I am born again. I am a new creation. I am born again. I am a new creation in Christ.

DAY SIX

THANK YOU FOR CALVARY

"And when they were come to the place, which is called Calvary, there they crucified him, and the malefactors, one on the right hand, and the other on the left." Luke 23:33

\#

Thank you, Jesus, for Calvary. Jesus, You died and shed your blood just for me. Your atonement, by the sacrifice on the cross, has set me free. KJV

OK

You paid the final redemption price for me. Jesus, you thought I was worth dying for, so you went to the cross just for me, to set me free.

Thank you, Jesus, for Calvary, the place where you died for me. Thank you for openly shedding your blood just to set me free.

At Mount Calvary, You personally came down from heaven as God so you could set me free.

Thank You, Jesus, for Calvary. You died on the cross just for me. You have set me free.

Scripture Reading On Personal Sacrifice of Jesus:
Matthew 27:33, Mark 15:22, Luke 23:33, John 19:17, Mark 15:22

I WORSHIP YOU

"Thou wilt shew me the path of life: in thy presence is fulness of joy; at thy right hand there are pleasures for evermore." Psalm 16:11

#

Lord, I worship You. I worship You and I adore You. Lord, from the bottom of my heart, I give you my praise.

I lift up my voice to worship You, O Lord. What a wonderful God that You are! You are always right here with me and never far away.

Your Word and your authority are settled in Heaven. I sing holy, holy, are You, Lord. I worship You for You are worthy to be Praised.

Scripture Reading on Worship:
Philippians 4:8, Jeremiah 29:11, John 3:16, Proverbs 4:23, Psalm 19:14, Psalm 16:11, Isaiah 58:1-4

TRUST AND OBEY

"Jesus answered and said unto him, If a man love me, he will keep my words; and my Father will love him, and we will come unto him, and make our abode with him." John 14:23

\#

God, I trust You because Your love is never-ending. Your love fills my heart every day. I trust you and I obey.

Your "word" guides me every day. I choose to trust You and I obey You. As they say, "There is no other way to be happy in You, Jesus, but to trust and obey."

I sing hallelujah…alleluia…because your Word is holy and true.

Lord, I trust and obey Your Word as part of the lifestyle I live every day.

Scripture Reading on Trusting God:
John 14:23, Deuteronomy 28:1, Proverbs 6:20, Deuteronomy 5:33, Proverbs 3:5-6.

DAY NINE

IN YOUR PRESENCE

"Bless the Lord, O my soul: and all that is within me, bless His holy name." Psalm 103:1

\#

In Your presence, I give my worship to You.

Lord, in Your presence, I have received my healing. Lord, in Your presence I worship You…for You are Jehovah Rapha, The GOD WHO HEALS.

Lord, in Your presence, I receive the fullness of joy. Lord, I rejoice in Your presence. Just to be in Your presence, my life is filled with joy, for you are my God.

You reign as Lord and King. You rule over everything. Oh, my heart rejoices in You! I sing my praise to You.

My heart sings praises. You are God and You are my King. Praises from my heart do I now sing. Songs of joy to You, my Savior and my King. Lord, I will honor You in everything that I do because my strength is in You.

Hallelujah! My praise is to You. In Your presence is where I want to be…joyful…happy…and set free. I sing my praise to You.

DAY TEN

Who is Your Best Friend

"Therefore we are buried with him by baptism into death: that like as Christ was raised up from the dead by the glory of the Father, even so we also should walk in newness of life."
Romans 6:4

\#

Has sin become your best friend? Does the obscure voice of sin speak secret messages from down within your heart? Does sin pretend to be your best friend? Leading you into the pathway of sin. Sin's voice says it will satisfy your soul from down within.

Does the survival of your thoughts only depend on the meditation of sin? Thinking that I must depend on my mind thinking about sin.

Satan is the father of sin. He always promises you the enjoyment of sin. Has sin become your best friend? Promising to stick by you to the end.

Has sin become your best friend? Does the voice of sin speak to your heart and divide you and God far apart? Does sin fill your heart?

Now it is time to repent and make Jesus your best friend. Let the precious blood of Jesus wash away your sin. It is time to stop letting Satan be your best friend. You must become born again so Jesus can set you free of sin. Accept Jesus as your best friend. Break friendship with sin. Invite Jesus in.

HOLY SPIRIT

"But the comforter which is the Holy Ghost, whom the Father will send in my name, he shall teach you all things, and bring all things to your remembrance, whatsoever I have said unto you." John 14:26

#

"Holy Spirit," come fill me. "Holy Spirit" please guide me every day.

"Holy Spirit," teach me to be all Jesus Christ wants me to be.

"Holy Spirit," come now and set my weary heart free.

"Holy Spirit," come resurrect God's holy standards inside of me.

"Holy Spirit," come set my mind and heart free.

"Holy Spirit" now lives inside of me.

** I Have Been Filled With The "Holy Spirit" for 39 years now!

Scripture Reading On The Holy Spirit:
Acts 1:8, John 14:26, John 15:26, 1 Corinthians 2:13, Ephesians 1:13, Ephesians 4:30, Acts 2:1-18.

Give Thanks

"Rejoice evermore." 17 "Pray without ceasing." 18 "In everything give thanks; for this is the will of God in Christ Jesus concerning you." 1 Thessalonians 5:16-18

#

I give you praise, honor, and Glory. Glory, Glory. Hallelujah! Thank you, Lord.

You're My Deliverer. My Defender. I Give you thanks for all You have done just for me.

You're victorious in every battle. You are a forever conquering King. God, I crown You with honor and glory, Righteous and heavenly King.

Thank you, Lord. I give glory and honor to You, my God, my King.

Thank You, Lord. My heart will praise You— forever, forever, forever my heart will praise you.

You bring me blessing upon blessing as heaven's door opens for me, for You work out everything for my good, for my good. For You are good all the time to me.

Your love covers me with Your goodness and mercy every day. I give you thanks for all that You have done for me. Your love covers me every day.

Scripture Reading on Giving Thanks:

1 Thessalonians 5:16-18, Psalm 103:1-4, Colossians 2:6-7, Isaiah 12:4-5, James 1:17, 1 Chronicles 16:34, Hebrews 12:28, Psalm 95:4-5

LORD, I BOW DOWN ON MY KNEES

"Submit yourselves therefore to God. Resist the Devil, and he will flee from you." 8 "Draw nigh to God, and He will draw nigh to you. Cleanse your hands, ye sinners, and purify your hearts, ye double-minded." James 4:7-8

#

Lord, now I bow down on my knees in prayer to You from the depths of my heart.

I pray to God, please set me free. I have so many chains of bondage now hanging on me.

Lord, set me free from being self-centered. Lord, set me free.

Lord, break these chains that hold me down from being the person that you want me to be.

I can no longer let my sin control me. Heaven, please help me. My soul is asking You to be free.

God send down Your holy miracle power at this very hour.

Lord, now I can feel Your resurrection power at this very hour working in me.

Thank you, Jesus, for sending me the victory...Your triumphant deliverance just for me. Now I am free.

DAY FOURTEEN

STILL THE SAME

"And you hath He quickened, who were dead in trespasses and sins; 2 "Wherein in time past ye walked according to the course of this world according to the prince of the power of the air, the spirit that now worketh in the children of disobedience." Ephesians 2:1-2

\#

Sadly, some people never want to change. Why are you still playing the same old sinful game of letting sin rule and reign in your own life?

Some things seem like they will never change.

Why do people like playing sin as a life game? Sin doesn't have to rule and reign in your life. Sin can make your life full of heartache and pain.

Still the same, blaming God for everything wrong. Don't blame God for all the things in your life that you do not want to change.

God is not the reason for all your heartache and pain. Your life of sin still stays the same…not wanting to change.

Stop living life only for self-centered prideful material gain. Jesus can change your heart and sin can be far apart. Invite Him to live in your heart. When you become born again, life will change.

Scripture Reading: We Can't Live In Sin:
Romans 1:22, Proverbs 21:2, Proverbs 24:12, Colossians 1:20-21, Ephesians 2:1, Titus 1:15-16, Romans 10:9-10

My Heart Trusts in You

"It is of the Lord's mercies that we are not consumed because His compassions fail not." 23 "They are new every morning; great is thy faithfulness." Lamentations 3:22-23

\#

My heart trusts in only You God, only You.

My heart, I now surrender to You.

With my heart, I have total trust in You.

My heart trusts in You, God.

Lord, I love You. I trust in You.

I'm placing all of my faith in You, God.

My heart trusts in You. All of my faith is in You, with my life, I trust You, only You.

I Sing Praises to You

"Saying with a loud voice, Worthy is the Lamb that was slain to receive power, and riches, and wisdom, and strength, and honor, and glory, and blessing." Revelation 5:12

#

I sing praises to Your name, with my heart, I sing praise to You, again and again.

I sing praise to You, my hope is always in You.

I sing praises to You. All of my worship is only to You.

I sing all my praises to You. I will give You all glory due to You, only to You.

You make my life new because my life is in You.

My hope and expectation is in You, Lord.

I sing praise to You—all the praise belongs to You. Glory and honor belong to You, only to You.

Scripture Reading On Praising God:
Revelation 5:12-13, Revelation 5:14, Revelation 4:8-10, Revelation 5:2-5, Revelation 5:8-10

LORD, HERE I AM

"I beseech you therefore, brethren, by the mercies of God, that ye present your bodies a living sacrifice, holy, acceptable unto God, which is your reasonable service." 2 "And be not conformed to this world, but be ye transformed by the renewing of your mind, that ye may prove what is that good, and acceptable, and perfect will of God." Romans 12:1-2

#

LORD, here I am. I'm all Yours, LORD God.

Let Your Holy Word cleanse my heart of everything that keeps us apart.

Holy Spirit, make me whole again. My heart is set free to worship You.

God, give me peace from the Holy Spirit within My Heart.

LORD, here I Am. LORD, here I am. I'm all Yours.

Teach me Your will and Your holy way to walk by Your side every day.

LORD, here I am. LORD, here I am, I'm all Yours.

I surrender my heart to You today and every day.

LORD, here I am. Use me to do Your will every day of my life.

LOVE DREAMS

"Who hath delivered us from the power of darkness, and hath translated us into the kingdom of his dear son:" 14 "In whom we have redemption through His blood, even the forgiveness of sins:" 15 "Who is the image of the invisible God, the firstborn of every creature:" Colossians 1:13-15

#

I lie down asleep and my mind begins to dream. I reach out to embrace God.
He is not there.
Emotions of fear entomb my mind, though fragmented by the passing of time.
I frantically search for Him, He is still not there.
Panic now fills my heart, frantically, I search for Him everywhere.
Then suddenly—coming from a distance, I hear a wonderful sound.
It is the beautiful voice of God…saying, I'm always here with you, my child, my son.
I will never leave you. My Spirit is always with you.
I begin to awaken, just to behold the dawning of the morning sun.
There is God's hand reaching out His hand to me. Suddenly, I feel God's love and tender mercy touching me.
And Jesus, setting me free. I heard Jesus speaking words of love, just to me.
My heart stood still as Jesus spoke ever so softly to me.
Love was no longer just a dream to me, the love of Jesus—my personal Savior—came to live inside of me. His Spirit now lives in me.

Scripture Reading on God's Love:
John 3:16, Colossians 1:13, Colossians 2:2-3, Ephesians 2:14-18, John 3:18-19

AT THE CROSS

"For God so loved the world, that he gave his only begotten Son, that whosoever believeth in him should not perish, but have everlasting life." John 3:16

#

At the cross, at the cross. Jesus my Savior, shed His own blood just for me.

At the cross is where Jesus gave sin its defeat, at the cross.

Jesus conquered Satan and stripped him of all his authority, at the cross, Jesus.

Jesus gave me victory now! The righteousness of Jesus, my perfect substitute, Jesus lives in me.

At the cross, Jesus set me free. New life now lives inside of me, the Spirit of God lives inside of me.

At the cross, at the cross, salvation was purchased by the blood of Jesus just for me. So He can come live in my heart personally.

DAY TWENTY

JESUS, YOU'RE MY DREAM COME TRUE

"And to know the love of Christ, which passeth knowledge, that ye might be filled with all the fullness of God."
Ephesians 3:19

\#

Last night, I lay down fast asleep, but my anxious heart stayed awake.

While in a dream state of mind, I heard a small still voice softly calling out my name personally; who could it be?

I thought maybe my heart was just anxious again, and I felt my heart beating faster.

My head raised up and turned around quickly just to see who it could be.

To my mind's amazement, it was You. The God who my heart personally now knew!

You stole my heart on the very first day that we met.

As I began to awaken out of my sleep, in my heart I came to realize that You are my heart's only dream come true. Jesus, I love You!

DAY TWENTY-ONE

HALLELUJAH!

"O Come, let us sing unto the Lord; let us make a joyful noise to the rock of our salvation." Psalm 95:1

#

Hallelujah! Hallelujah!

I praise You, I thank You, my glorious King.

You bring me the fullness of joy when my heart is full of sadness.

Your Holy Spirit brings my soul gladness.

Hallelujah! No more sadness. Now my heart overflows with praise.

LORD, my heart now fills up with Your Love.

With my lips, I will praise you.

Hallelujah! Hallelujah!

You are worthy to be praised. My hands are raised up to You.

Hallelujah!

Scripture Reading on Worshiping God:
Psalm 95:1, Psalm 95:2, Psalm 95:3-6

JESUS

Philippians 2:10 "At the name of Jesus, every knee shall bow, of things in heaven, and things of earth, and things under the earth." Philippians 2:10

#

Who are You? You are JESUS, name above all names.

Your name is wonderful. That's who You are.

Your name is Mighty God, Almighty God That's who You are.

You Are Everlasting Peace. That's who You are.

God, You are All-Powerful, Prince of Peace.

JESUS, Sweet Jesus. Name above all names.

Forever merciful, Loving God. God of mercy.

Abba Father, You are to me. No longer an orphan, I am Yours for eternity.

You are forever The Prince of Peace, Jesus, sweet Jesus, Righteousness, King Jesus, Jesus, name above all Names. God and King, That is who You are!

Scripture Reading on Jesus:
Philippians 2:10, Isaiah 9:6, Acts 4:33, Colossians 1:33, James 4:6-7, 1 Thessalonians 5:18

SIN IS NO GAME

"For the wages of sin is death, but the gift of God is eternal life through Jesus Christ our Lord." Romans 6:23

#

Do you think that sin is a game? Playing a life and living in sin is no game.

It only invites the devil, the father of sin, to come into your life.

He wants to stand by your side as your best friend.

Why? Because fellowship with your favorite sin will soon bring the spirit of disobedience into your life...which causes a life of strife with God.

It's time to make a change. Repentance is to change—it is freedom from the bondage of sin. You must be born again, by His Spirit, to be free of sin.

Scripture Reading on we all have Sinned:
Romans 6:23, Romans 3:23, Romans 5:6, Rom 6:14, 2 Corinthians 5:17, Acts 4:12, Ephesians 2:1-5

I Love You, Lord

"The Lord is my portion, saith my soul, therefore will I hope in Him." Lamentations 3:24

\#

I love You, LORD, for your faithfulness is never failing.

I love You, LORD, Your promises in Your Word never fail. You watch over your Word and perform miracles for me… just for me.

I love You, LORD. Your mercy and grace I daily receive, Your love is ever-flowing, touching me.

I love You, Lord!

Scripture Reading on Your love never fails:
Psalm 136, Lamentations 3:22

HEAL ME, O GOD!

"Heal me O Lord, and I shall be healed, save me and I shall be saved, for thou art my praise." Jeremiah 17:14

\#

Heal Me O God! You are the God who always heals.

Heal me, O LORD! You are the God who forever heals us.

You're my Deliverer in times of trouble.

Heal me, O LORD! You are the God Who heals. You are never changing.

You give miracles freely each and every day.

By Your stripes, I am now healed.

Matthew's Testimony—I have been 100% healed of leukemia for six years now by God!

Scripture Reading on Healing:
Jeremiah 17:14, Isaiah 41:10, I Peter 2:24, Jeremiah 33:6, Isaiah 53:5, Psalm 41:3. James 5:15, 3 John 2

LET GO!

"Casting all your care upon Him, for He careth for you."
1 Peter 5:7

\#

Let go… of the past.

Let go… of all your hurts and fears.

Let go… and let God heal… heal you of everything.

Let go… of all worldly desires… because God's ways are higher than our ways… earthly things will soon pass away… only eternal things will last forever.

Let go… and let God be God… let Him do a miracle today.

Let go… and let God take away your hurt and pain. Let go of your Sorrow Today.

And Let God heal you… God hears you when you pray… reach out to God today.

I am Redeemed

"Grace be to you and peace from God the Father, and from our Lord, Jesus Christ."

4. "Who gave himself for our sins, that he might deliver us from this present evil world, according to the will of God and our Father." Galatians 1:3-4

#

My praises are to You, God… I am redeemed!

I am no longer a prisoner of sin. Through the blood of Jesus, I have been cleansed of my sin.

No longer can Satan have authority over me. Jesus redeemed me… He paid the price to set me free.

The Holy Spirit showed me the Truth, and the Truth has set me free… Praise Jesus! Satan has no authority over me.

I am redeemed.

Scripture Reading on being redeemed:
Galatians 1:4, Galatians 2:20, Galatians 3:13, Hebrews 9:15, Isaiah 44:22, 2 Peter 3:9, Acts 3:19

DAY TWENTY-EIGHT

LORD, I GIVE UP DOING THINGS MY WAY

"For what is a man profited, if he shall gain the whole world, and lose his own soul? or what shall a man give in exchange for his soul?" Matthew 16:26

#

LORD, I surrender my life to You, today.

I choose to no longer do things my own way.

Lord, teach me how to walk Your holy and righteous way… walk the narrow pathway, the way which leads to life.

LORD, I deny myself and my sinful ways today.

LORD, I surrender to You my life today. I give You my life today.

I give You my life today… I choose to no longer do things my own way.

LORD, I choose to obey Your word and everything You say.

In my heart, I choose to follow Your will and Your way.

LORD, I surrender to You… to do Your will today and every day… I surrender my heart today.

DAY TWENTY-NINE

I WAITED ON YOU

"Wait on the Lord: be of good courage, and he shall strengthen thine heart: wait, I say, on the Lord." Psalm 27:14

\#

I waited patiently on You, Lord. I called out to You in my distress.

You heard my cry with pain in my chest God. Why is my life a big mess?

With Your right hand of mighty power, You reached down and rescued me.

Lord, thank You for always getting me out of the messes I get in.

King of Glory, All praises belong to You.

I waited patiently on You, Lord. All the honor belongs to You. All the glory belongs to You.

God all praises to Your name. I waited patiently on You, Lord.

You delivered me and You answered me. You came right there when I called, to answer my prayer.

DAY THIRTY

It's Time to Pray

"Be careful for nothing, but in everything by prayer and supplication with thanksgiving let your requests be made known unto God. 7 And the peace of God, which passeth all understanding, shall keep your hearts and minds through Christ Jesus." Philippians 4:6-7

\#

It is time to pray to God today.

I bow down and worship You, God, today.

It is time to put my anxious thoughts away.

It is time to pray today. Let my mind meditate on Your Word today.

Lord, I need Your holy presence today. I need You in every way.

It is time to pray today. Lord, purify my heart today…cleanse me.

Let your perfect love abound in my heart today. Look upon me with Your eyes of mercy because I need You today.

You are the Savior of the world. You are the Lord of all. Thank You, Lord, for catching me when I fall.

Lord, thank You for answering my prayer today. I cannot express all my heart wants to say…I love You more every day.

DAY THIRTY-ONE

JESUS LOVES ME ANYWAY

"And said, O Lord God of Israel, there is no God like thee in the heaven, nor in the earth, which keepest covenant, and shewest mercy unto thy servants, that walk before thee with all their hearts." 2 Chronicles 6:14

\#

Jesus loves me anyway…even when I personally fail Him every day.

Jesus loves me anyway.

I feel His love as I now bow down to pray even though I don't know what to say.

Jesus loves me anyway.

Even when I feel too weak to pray. Jesus loves me anyway.

He loves me more every single day even when I fail Him in so many ways.

I'M TRUSTING IN JESUS EVERY DAY IN FAITH

"Trust in the LORD with all thine heart; and lean not unto thine own understanding. 6 In all thy ways acknowledge him, and he shall direct thy paths." Proverbs 3:5-6

#

I'm believing God's Word every day…He is guiding my life every day.

I feel my faith growing stronger every day…God chased all my doubts out of the way.

When life's troubles come my way…I have learned to get down on my knees and pray and trust Him every day.

Trusting Jesus every day…trusting in Jesus every day… God is a God of Miracles…working miracles every day.

I just believe and have faith and He makes a way out of no way.

Trusting in Jesus every day…God, I rely on You in every way of life…every day.

You are faithful…Faithful God, are You.

You are good all the time…your joy fills my heart.

I love you, God and I trust You every day…I trust You every day…You make a way out of no way.

Scripture Reading about Trusting God:

Proverbs 3:5-6, Psalm 37:4-5, Psalm 33:20, Isaiah 26:3, Isaiah 12:2, Psalm 9:10

DID YOU LISTEN TO WHAT GOD HAS TO SAY?

13 "Howbeit when he, the Spirit of truth, is come, he will guide you into all truth: for he shall not speak of himself; but whatsoever he shall hear, that shall he speak: and he will shew you things to come." 14 "He shall glorify me: for he shall receive of mine and shall shew it unto you." John 16:13-14

\#

Did you listen to what God has to say today?.. While you were down on your knees to pray.

Did you listen to what God has to say in His Word today?...Or did you let doubt and sin get in the way?

Did you listen to what God has to say today? God is always speaking in His Word every day.

If you just listen to him when you pray…You will hear his still small voice today…It's the voice of love.

His love is surrounding you every day… His love surrounds you every day…Do you hear Him? He speaks of love every day.

Scripture Reading on Listening to God:
Romans 12:1-2, Romans 9:1, John 14:26, John 16:13

DAY THIRTY-FOUR

SPIRIT OF DEPRESSION

17 "The righteous cry, and the Lord heareth, and delivereth them out of all their troubles. 18 The Lord is nigh unto them that are of a broken heart; and saveth such as be of a contrite spirit." Psalm 34:17-18

#

Depression and eternal darkness seem to always follow me.

Oh God, my peace of mind…where can it be?

Why God, does my peace of mind seem to run from me?

Fear and worry now rage in my mind.

My thoughts toss like the waves of the sea.

Oh God, no guiding light do I now see anywhere around me.

Because depression guides me…I cry out to You, God.

You send Your holy presence to set me free.

Now depression no longer has a hold on me.

I can now lie down…I have peace and I can now sleep… Depression is gone from me.

DAY THIRTY-FIVE

JESUS LIFTED ME

"If the Son therefore shall make you free, ye shall be free indeed." John 8:36

#

Jesus Lifted Me…from the bondage of sin, Jesus set me free.

Jesus lifted me…no more bondage can I now see.

Jesus lifted me…I am born again and I am free…no more chains holding me.

Jesus lifted me…In God there is liberty and freedom in His presence…there we can be free.

Jesus lifted me…Jesus set me free…Jesus lifted me…His holy power can deliver me every hour.

In His name, there is deliverance power.

I DELIGHT MYSELF IN YOU

"Delight thyself also in the Lord: and he shall give thee the desires of thine heart." Psalm 37:4

\#

I delight myself in You, God...I know in my heart Your Word is true.

I delight myself in You, my God and redeemer.

My heart takes pleasure in knowing You...I surrender and humble my heart to You.

I delight myself in You...I know in my heart that Your Word is true.

I delight myself in You...I love only You...God of truth and all knowledge.

My heart takes pleasure in knowing You...God Your word is truth...I acknowledge You in everything that I do.

I love You and my heart will sing Your praise. My soul acknowledges You.

Scripture Reading on Delighting in God:
Psalm 37:4, Psalm 1:1-6, Psalm 43:3, Psalms 138:3, Psalm 34:4, Zephaniah 3:17

THE MAN IN THE MIRROR

For if any be a hearer of the word and not a doer, he is like unto a man beholding his natural face in a glass." James 1:23

#

I'm looking at the man in the mirror…now all I see is a sinful man looking back at me.

Why God, can I not have peace of mind?

That old man of sin just keeps looking at me.

Why will he not just let me be? I just want to enjoy a life of sin and live free.

I am looking at the old man in the mirror.

and no peace can I see…my mind can't get free.

I wish that old man of sin would just stop staring back at me.

(Continued on the next page.)

CONTINUED

Why does he just let me be me? Just enjoying sin and living life free.

Now I look in the mirror…that old man of sin is still staring back at me.

Why does he keep following me? He will not let me be me…loving sin and only living just for me.

Now I can hear the voice of sin speaking to me…because that old man of sin keeps tempting me.

God, I now get down on my knees…saying God, forgive me of all my sins. I want to be born again.

Please take that old man of sin away from me so I can have peace.

Scripture Reading on living according to the flesh:
James 1:23, Romans 12:1-2, Romans 7:5, Romans 7:23, Romans 8:7, Galatians 3:26-29

REDEMPTION

"In whom we have redemption through his blood, the forgiveness of sins, according to the riches of his grace."
Ephesians 1:7

#

I am redeemed…I am no longer a prisoner of sin because Jesus died on the cross for me.

Your precious blood has set us totally free…You are the awesome Creator of this world.

God, Your Holy Spirit now lives in me.

Your love is working continually inside of me showing me that I am loved continually.

You have redeemed me…I am no longer a prisoner of sin.

The blood of Jesus has cleansed me from my sin.

I am redeemed…You bought me with a price.

Jesus paid with His life on the cross to redeem me back from the captivity of Satan and sin.

Scripture Reading on Redemption:
Ephesians 1:7, Galatians 1:4, Galatians 2:20, Galatians 3:13,
Hebrews 9:15. Isaiah 44:22, 1 Peter 3:9, Acts 3:19

WHAT IS SALVATION AND BEING BORN AGAIN?

"That if thou shalt confess thy mouth the Lord Jesus, and shalt believe in thine heart that God hath raised him from the dead, thou shalt be saved." Romans 10:9

#

The saving grace of Jesus Christ...the Bible says there is only one way to heaven.

Jesus said I am The Way...The Truth and The Life...no man comes unto the Father but by Me. (John 3:16)

No one else can save you...trust Jesus today.

If thou shalt confess with thy mouth the Lord Jesus and shalt believe in thine heart that God hath raised Him from the dead...thou shalt be saved. (Romans 10:9)

Be willing to repent... (Acts 17:30)

Admit that you are a sinner... (Romans 3:10)

(Continued on the next page.)

DAY THIRTY-NINE

CONTINUED

Believe that Jesus died just for You and was buried and rose from the dead… (Romans 10:9-10).

Pray this prayer NOW…Dear God, I am a sinner and I need your forgiveness.

I believe that Jesus Christ died and shed His blood for my sins…I repent and turn away from my sins.

I now invite Jesus into my heart to be my Lord and Savior now…LORD, I give you my life today.

TEMPTATION

"There hath no temptation taken you but such as is common to man: but God is faithful, who will not suffer you to be tempted above that ye are able; but will with the temptation also make a way to escape, that ye may be able to bear it." Corinthians 10:13

\#

Why does sin tempt me with lustful desires?

Temptation to sin…I am lured by things that my eyes see.

Sinful desires keep coming up at me…a picture of sin do my eyes see.

Lustful desires are tempting me…I pray God…Please help me now!

I thank You, God, You are faithful and make a way to escape every temptation.

Thank You, God, You give me victory to overcome desires that rise up inside of me.

Sin has no control over me…victory over temptation belongs to me.

I am depending on You, Jesus to help me stay free.

Scripture Reading on Temptation:
1 Corinthians 10:13, James 1:12-14, Luke 22:40, John 8:6, Matthew 6:13, Mark 8:11, Matthew 22:18

THE LORD, THE GREAT I AM

"And God said unto Moses, I AM THAT I AM: and he said, Thus shall thou say unto the children of Israel, I AM hath sent me unto you." Exodus 3:14

#

God is Jehovah-Rapha…You are The LORD Who Heals (Exodus 15:26).

God is Jehovah-Nissi…You are The LORD Our Banner (Exodus 17:15).

God is Jehovah Raah…The LORD My Shepherd… (Psalm 23:1).

God is Jehovah Tsidkenu…The LORD our Righteousness…(Jeremiah 23:6).

God is Jehovah Shammah…The LORD is There… (Ezekiel 48:35).

God is El Shaddai…The GOD Who is More Than Enough…(Genesis 17:1).

Scripture Reading on The Names of God:
Genesis 22:14, Exodus 15:26, Exodus 17:15, Psalm 23:1, Jeremiah 23:6, Ezekiel 48:35, Genesis 17:1

I Lift My Hands to Praise You

"Thus will I bless thee while I live: I will lift up my hands in thy name." Psalm 63:4

\#

I lift up my hands to praise You, Jesus.

Emanuel, God Is With Us…for You are worthy to be praised.

You are worthy…So worthy, O Lord.

I lift up my hands and I praise You…for You are worthy to be praised.

Your mercy and Your goodness endures forever.

All the days of my life I will forever praise You…for You are worthy to be praised.

I clap my hands…I lift up my voice…because You, O LORD, are worthy to be Praised…today and every day.

Your mercy endures forever…I will forever praise You… I lift my voice to praise You.

Scripture Reading on Praising God:
Psalm 63:4, Psalm 134:2, Psalm 141:2

DAY FORTY-THREE

PRAISE TO YOU

"Let everything that hath breath praise the Lord. Praise ye the Lord." Psalm 150:6

\#

Hallelujah! Hallelujah!

Lord, I give You praise and with my dance I praise You.

I will sing praises to You as long as I live…O Lord, You are great…You are greatly to be praised.

I will sing my praise to You, My God…for You are clothed in majesty.

I give You honor, for Your kingdom authority.

God, You reign…You reign…and You are greatly to be praised…I praise Your holy name.

Hallelujah! Hallelujah!

Your goodness and mercy endure forever…from my heart, I shout for joy…

Because You are God…Who always gives me victory…in every situation that tries to overtake me… You give me victory.

So I shout for joy…I sing praise to You…I dance in freedom praising You.

You Chose Me

"But ye are a chosen generation, a royal priesthood, an holy nation, a peculiar people; that ye should shew forth the praises of him who hath called you out of darkness into his marvelous light." 1 Peter 2:9

#

You came into my life…You chose me.

You God, personally called me to follow You on the day we first met.

You reached out Your arms of love to me to express how much You love me.

I heard You calling me by my name.

You took all of my sinful shame.

You removed all of my pain.

You came and bought me a new life…You chose me.

You reached Your hands out to me.

(Continued on the next page.)

DAY FORTY-FOUR

Your Word leads me to the knowledge of how You can set me free…You chose me.

You personally came to me.

You said…My son, follow Me.

You said I will teach you how to walk holy and free…You chose me.

You chose me to be a royal priest.

You called me out of darkness…into the light of Your kingdom…You chose me.

When I could not see….You opened my eyes and Your love set me free.

Scripture Reading on being called by God:
1 Peter 2:9, Matthew 22:14, 2 Timothy 1:9

WHAT IS CHRISTMAS ABOUT?

"For God so loved the world, that he gave his only begotten Son, that whosoever believeth in him should not perish, but have everlasting life." John 3:16

\#

What a wonderful and glorious day!

It is a day when Father God, Who lives in heaven, sent down His Son Jesus Christ.

Jesus, our perfect sacrifice…on the cross, He gave us grace and salvation.

By His death and resurrection, He gave us freedom from sin and set us free from Satan's hand.

Once we are born again, Jesus comes into our hearts and becomes our best friend; Jesus our perfect sacrifice.

By His own blood, he paid sin's final price in order to bring us out of darkness into God's marvelous kingdom of light.

God in heaven gives us a new life. His love comes to live in our hearts…His love wraps around us and holds us tight.

On the day of Christmas, Jesus is always shining as heaven's light.

My Confession of Faith in God

Greater is Jesus who lives in me than the devil in the world.

I am filled with the divine love of God which flows through me.

No weapon formed against me will prosper…I am an overcomer.

I am victorious.

Jesus is greater than all the works of the devil.

I am fearless because Jesus lives in me.

I walk in victory in Jesus Christ now.

About the Author

Matthew Wallace was born in Tulsa Oklahoma in 1960. His father had a 55-year successful career as a Baptist preacher in several different churches before he passed on to heaven in 2004. Matthew grew up as a church-going child with one older brother and four older sisters, raised in a wonderful Christian family.

For the first 18 years of his life, Matthew did not personally know Jesus Christ. On April 15, 1979, he repented of his sins and said the sinner's prayer while watching Pat Robertson on The 700 Club.

God and the Holy Spirit took him on a trip to see the gates of hell. He fell down into a pitch-black hole for what seemed like many miles and many hours. He heard people screaming and crying. It was so hot he was sweating. His eyes saw fire shooting up at the gates of hell…very high flames. He saw ugly horrible giant creatures standing at the gates of hell. He heard terrible wailing from the people… their voices filled his ears.

He almost fell into hell, but a huge hand came down and caught him. Matthew was safe in God's hands. God lifted him out of hell on April 15, 1979, at 2:00 p.m.

Being rescued from hell, he was free of hate, anger, and

bondage. That was the day he was born again.

Right after that spiritual experience with God, he started taking correspondence Bible school classes. Throughout the past forty-three years, he has completed training in seven Bible schools through home correspondence and churches in his hometown. Thirty-nine years ago, Matthew was filled with the Holy Spirit and began speaking in tongues from God.

The Holy Spirit inspired him to write this short book of poems. This book is dedicated to God and is intended to give glory to God.

Matthew desires for people to know who God is in His character and personality. He is all-sufficient and will provide everything we need.

This collection of short gospel poems speaks of God's saving grace and almighty power.

God is holy. Matthew's gospel poems are designed to express the eternal attributes of who God is to us. The purpose of this book is to declare God's glory.